OPERATIONAL RISK MANAGEMENT:
Simple Reflections on Operational Risk Management for Success

Joseph S. Slack

All rights reserved. No part of this publication may be reproduced, distributed, or transmitted in any form or by any means, including photocopying, recording, or other electronic or mechanical methods, without the prior written permission of the publisher, except in the case of brief quotations embodied in critical reviews and certain other noncommercial uses permitted by copyright law.

Copyright © Joseph S. Slack, 2022.

Table of content

Chapter 1

Operational Risk Management

Operational risk management (ORM) is a continuous, repeatable process that involves risk assessment, risk decision-making, and the application of risk controls, to accept, reduce, or avoid risk.

Every firm has events or fundamental shifts in its environment that might pose varying degrees of risk to that business, from small annoyances to a predicament that could endanger the whole enterprise.

Operational risk examples include:

employee behavior and employee mistake

Private data breach brought on by cyberattacks
Automation, robotics, and artificial intelligence-related technology hazards
Organizational procedures and controls
Physical occurrences like natural catastrophes that might interfere with company operations.

Fraud both within and outside
Operational risk is defined as "the risk of loss coming from insufficient or failing internal processes, people, and systems, or external events" by the Basel Committee on Banking Supervision.

As a result, operational risk includes hazards associated with business continuity plans, the environment, crisis management, process systems, and operations, as well as risks associated with people, their health and safety, and information technology.

The topic of operational risk management is often brought up concerning financial services.

Organizations that seek to prevent potentially catastrophic problems must have an operational risk management methodology.

Advantages of ORM
One of a company's primary advantages of operational risk management is that it can:

Boost the consistency of its corporate operations
Boost the efficiency of its risk management activities.
Whenever there are dangers involved, decision-making should be strengthened.
Reduce losses brought on by improperly categorized risks.
Detect illegal activity quickly
lower expenses for compliance

lessen the possible harm from foreseeable dangers

A corporation may accomplish its strategic goals while maintaining business continuity in the case of operational interruptions by establishing an efficient operational risk management program.

Strong organizational risk management practices can demonstrate to clients that the business is ready to handle losses and calamities. Successfully implementing a strong organizational risk management program may provide organizations with better competitive advantages, such as:

an increase in C-suite visibility
better knowledge while incurring business risks
enhanced product functionality and increased brand familiarity
improved connections with stakeholders and consumers
more optimistic investors

more accurate performance reporting
Financial forecasting that is more sustainable

Operational risk management stages:
Finding risks
risk evaluation
mitigation and measurement
reporting and observation

Risk Identification
Understanding the nature of the business and the possible risks related to that firm is the first step in developing an operational risk management plan. Employees from all divisions of the company should be involved in risk assessment, if at all feasible.

Risk Evaluation
The organization must evaluate the risks after they have been identified. Companies must accomplish this while using both a quantitative and qualitative approach, taking into account variables like occurrence

frequency and intensity. According to these parameters, the evaluation must give management of these risks top priority.

Mitigation and Measurement
The next step is to reduce or eliminate these dangers. Organizations must implement controls to reduce their exposure to risks and the potential harm these risks may cause. Managers may avoid losses by using metrics like key risk indicators (KRIs).

Reporting and Monitoring
A procedure for continuous monitoring and reporting of these risks must be in place for any operational risk management strategy, in part to show how successful the plan has been. This procedure should guarantee that the solutions put in place are still controlling the risks and are still effective.

The C-suite may employ good risk management skills as a critical tool to acquire a competitive edge and enable improved business decision-making.

Risk managers are aware of the value they provide to any firm and the purpose of their position. However, other workers may be unaware of what the risk department performs or the broad advantages of their approach and deeds. They could sometimes be unable to articulate risk management precisely! This leads to difficulty.

When risk management is not widely understood, it is more difficult for risk managers to get support for the implementation of mitigation measures. Here are reasons why risk management is important that all workers should consider. Please spread the word to your team about this!

Reasons Why Risk Management Is Important for Every Employee

1. Everyone must control risk.
There are hazards in any organization. The majority of businesspeople are fully aware that success sometimes necessitates taking risks. Even yet, risk management is sometimes seen as "the department of no" — those who reject any project proposal that seems to have any possible risks. The reality is the exact reverse of this.

Not all hazards are meant to be eliminated as part of risk management. It is to reduce the possible negative effects of hazards. Employees that collaborate with risk managers may take calculated risks that increase the likelihood of return.

2. Risk management improves workplace safety

Critical facets of a risk manager's job include health and safety. They actively search for organizational issue areas and try to solve them. They employ data analysis to find patterns in losses and injuries, then put prevention measures in place to stop them from happening again.

This helps workers in physically demanding occupations like construction, but it may also assist office workers and others in comparable roles via strategies like ergonomics. Risk management has a significant influence on workplace safety and is better for everyone.

3. Risk management promotes the success of projects

Risk managers may support staff members in their initiatives, regardless of the department. They may do the same for individual projects in the same way that they evaluate risks and create strategies to optimize corporate performance. By early risk identification, staff members may lessen the possibility and severity of prospective project hazards. There will be a plan of action in place in case anything does go wrong. Employees may do this to prepare for the unexpected and improve project results.

4. Risk management minimizes unplanned incidents

Most people dislike surprises, especially when they affect their workplace. The objective of a risk manager is to identify all potential risks, map them out, and then work to minimize or eliminate them.

Even though it's impossible to anticipate every risk scenario and address it, a risk manager reduces the likelihood and severity of unpleasant surprises. When it appears like anything significant may go wrong, an employee should speak to the risk manager or the risk management department first. There's a significant probability that it already has a plan in place.

5. Risk management brings about monetary gains

The organization's risk management division shouldn't be seen as a cost center. In actuality, it generates value immediately. Risk managers may identify high-frequency incidents and take action to reduce recurring losses by using trend analysis. When accidents do happen, they will happen less often and will have less of an effect, possibly saving the company thousands, if not millions, of dollars.

The professionals who get the proper amounts of insurance to optimize the financial effect of the risk management program are risk managers.

6. Risk management reduces work and saves time
When events happen, staff members of all levels take time to report data to the risk management division.
These duties are often carried out inefficiently and piecemeal. The risk department can relieve workers of the pressure of tiresome data entry by simplifying these activities, freeing them up to devote time and effort to their actual jobs.

It is simple for staff members to support high ROI risk management activities, facilitate risk managers' tasks, and enjoy the advantages of a formal risk management program when a sound procedure is in place.

Risk management enhances communication, point seven.

The well-being of a business and its employees depends on both horizontal and vertical communication. They encourage awareness of both internal and external challenges and facilitate productive teamwork. Even if most workers are aware of this, the implementation may be challenging if certain parties are unaware of the potential consequences.

Risk managers might be useful. By acting as a single point of contact for all risk data and disseminating reports and analyses, they facilitate horizontal communication. By establishing expectations and connecting information to company objectives, risk managers foster vertical communication. Employees gain from extra communication channels.

8. Risk management guards against reputation concerns.

Numerous dangers entail a reputational risk or an event that would make the public think poorly of the company. Even if they were not directly engaged, reputational problems might nevertheless affect certain workers. An official risk department significantly reduces the chance of this consequence.

A systematic risk management program and methods will effectively contain an incident when it inevitably happens and reduce the likelihood of an escalation and broad-based negative effects.

9. Cultural advantages of risk management
All parties—frontline employees, risk managers, executives, and decision-makers—benefit from a strong risk management culture. It fosters a culture of safety and prevention that penetrates the company and affects how workers behave. It establishes performance standards and

projects a favorable image to the general public.

10. Risk management directs the choice
Making decisions may be difficult, particularly when those decisions will have a big influence on future performance. Employees may be guided by risk management data and analytics to make good strategic choices that will help the organization achieve its goals.

Additionally, they may provide advice on the advantages and disadvantages of a choice option and suggest which risks should be taken and which should be avoided. The risk management division is a great resource for advice for staff members across the board.

Any employee who works with risk managers should have a newfound understanding as a result of this knowledge, which will also assist to increase organizational buy-in for risk management activities. Use it to get people behind risk management goals or to get any of the advantages listed above.

Operational risk: what is it?
Operational risk is the danger of suffering losses as a result of poor or ineffective procedures, rules, plans, or circumstances that interfere with business operations. Operational risk can be caused by a variety of factors, including employee mistakes, criminal activity like fraud, and natural disasters.

The majority of organizations recognize that mistakes will inevitably be made by their personnel and operational procedures. Practical corrective measures should be highlighted in the evaluation of operational risk to reduce exposures and guarantee effective responses.

Operational risk may result in financial loss, a competitive disadvantage, issues with employees or customers, and even company collapse if it is not handled.

identifying and reducing operational risk
Which factors give rise to operational risk?
People within or outside of the organization, technology, processes, or even outside events, such as the following, can be the root of operational risk.
governing, managing risks, and complying (GRC)
risk reduction
risk chart (risk heat map)
Natural disasters like earthquakes, hurricanes, or wildfires; global health crises like the COVID-19 pandemic; man-made disasters like terrorism, cyberterrorism, and cybercrime; negligence and other workplace-related torts like sexual harassment, a hostile work environment,

discrimination, etc.; regulatory compliance violations, breach of contract, antitrust, market manipulation, and unfair trade practices.

The majority of operational risks are often caused by individuals and actions made by people (human error).

What kind of operational hazards are there? The following consequences are possible as a result of the aforementioned operational risk causes:

Enterprise-wide disruption, failure, or interruption; loss of system control or data; financial loss, including denial of an insurance claim; safety risks; reputational damage; IT infrastructure damage; customer churn; employee churn; legal liability or regulatory fines for harm caused by employees intentionally or negligently; legal liability or regulatory fines for harm

caused by external bad actors; and competitive disadvantage.
Listed here are the Basel II event categories.

How are operational risk metrics calculated? To quantify operational risk, key risk indicators (KRIs) and data are often needed. However, the measurement may be particularly difficult when businesses are unable to combine all the many forms of data needed to comprehend their operational risk.

This may be caused, among other things, by data silos built by organizational fiefdoms or the lack of software that facilitates the collecting and analysis of data from various systems.

various operational risk types
Operational risk managers should continuously monitor and analyze risks in

real-time to reduce their potential effect as firms become more digital and use more data.

What primary risk indicators ought businesses monitor? That is dependent on the sector in which they work. For instance, banks adhere to recommendations made by the Basel Committee on Banking Supervision (BCBS), which outlines methods for calculating operational risk and mandates that banks set aside a certain amount of capital to protect against operational risk losses. Not all methods are perfect, however, businesses may quantify operational risk in the following ways:

monitoring important risk indicators, using statistical methods, employing scorecards, and doing scenario assessments in collaboration with risk management specialists and business specialists to assess the cost and likelihood of certain hazards;

Assessing brand reputational harm brought on by the risk, such as a data leak or breach that exposed customer data to unauthorized parties, tracking customer complaints, reviewing regulatory penalties from purposefully – or, more often, unintentionally – neglecting to notify or breaking a requirement.

Categories of Basel II events
The second of BCBS's three Basel Accords, Basel II is a collection of international banking rules that was first published in 2004.

Basel III, which was formed in direct reaction to the financial crisis, will take effect in January 2023. The seven operational risk categories listed under Basel II are as follows:

Internal theft Asset misappropriation, tax evasion, purposeful position misrepresentation, and bribery.

external deception Information theft, cyberattack damage, third-party theft, and forgeries.

safety in the workplace and employment procedures. Worker health and safety, workers' compensation, and discrimination. Customers, goods, and business procedures. Market manipulation, antitrust violations, unethical business practices, product flaws, fiduciary violations, and account churning.

Damage to material possessions terrorism, vandalism, and natural calamities.

System failures and business disruption. hardware issues, software malfunctions, and utility outages.

Delivery, process management, and execution. Errors in data entry and accounting, failure to submit required reports, and careless misappropriation of client assets.

Assessing operational risk is difficult.

Given the following, assessing and managing operational risk can be challenging:

The necessary information is not easily accessible.

Enterprises are becoming more operationally complicated.

The range of operational risk categories grows.

A sign of operational risks expanding definition is the overlap it has with other risk tasks.

What seems to be a duplicate risk function makes other risk functions feel threatened and prevents them from cooperating.

The operations crew laments that monitoring and reporting consume too much of their time.

How does operational risk management work?

While some firms don't, others do have a structured operational risk management department. They are often seen in people who are at various stages of development. However, these are the procedures businesses adhere to:

Define the scope, aim, and purpose of operational risk management. Keep in mind that different industries have different definitions of operational risk.

Define the roles that are essential to the function's success; these roles may or may not include a chief operational risk officer. Together with those other functions, define operational risk management's relationship to other risk management functions.

Choose the methods for measuring and monitoring operational risk.

Determine which tools will be required to support a successful operational risk function and if the company currently has such tools or whether more are needed. To prevent adding unneeded risk to the tech stack or unintentionally creating security vulnerabilities, only purchase what is essential with the aid of IT and security.

Establish secure access to the data required for operational risk management. Identify the appropriate data sources and their owners.

Identify process-related risks and their corresponding causes by working with other risk departments and the company.

Determine the processes' associated risks, such as their ability to scale as required or their suitability for the environment in which they operate.

Set up categories for risk.

Processes, hazards, and controls should all be well-mapped out.

Define the main risk markers.

Make sure all organization members involved in a process have been identified.

Recognize the resources needed for a procedure. Keep an eye out for adjustments, such as the need to scale down or up.

Know the company's risk tolerance in great detail.

Put control mechanisms in place.

Inform the employees of operational hazards and individual expectations. Include contact details so staff members will know who to speak with if there is a problem.

Determine the operational risk management function's influence on the company, and if the change is involved, make sure good change management procedures are followed.

Measure and keep an eye on operational hazards constantly. To identify trends, weak points, etc., use historical data.

Chapter 2

Diminishing People Risk

Identifying risk is an important first step. However, this is insufficient.
Taking precautions to mitigate risk is a must. Knowing about and thinking about risk is not the same as acting on risk.

There will be a risk. Some good, some bad. Some are minor, others are disastrous. Your ability to mitigate risk enables you to proactively recognize and accommodate risks. Let's look at four risk-mitigation strategies: avoidance, acceptance, reduction/control, and transfer.

Avoidance

If a risk has an unfavorable outcome, you may be able to completely avoid it. You can successfully avoid the occurrence of unwanted events by stepping away from the business activities involved or designing out the causes of the risk.

One way to avoid risk is to exit the business, cancel the project, close the factory, and so on. This has other consequences, but it is an option.

Another approach is to create policies and procedures that help the organization anticipate and avoid high-risk situations. By not starting a project with a high unwanted risk, you successfully avoid that risk.

Testing or screening products that may have a latent defect that could lead to unwanted and unacceptable high-field failures is an option. Although screening is not completely effective, it can significantly reduce the risk of field failures.

Design elements that allow an unwanted risk to occur out of a product or process. A product design change to a more robust material prevents unwanted failures caused by unacceptable wear of a less robust material. Implementing engineering design reviews in the product lifecycle process may aid in identifying high-risk areas of a new product or process before the decision to begin shipping.

Acceptance

Every product manufactured has a finite chance of failing in the hands of your customer. When that risk is at an acceptable level, with a sufficiently low estimated field failure rate, ship the product. Accept the risk.

When a decision to accept risk is based in part on an estimate or prediction, there is a risk that the information forecasts the future incorrectly. As a result, for high-impact field failures, closely monitoring field performance or establishing early warning systems may be prudent.

Control or reduction

FMEA, hazard analysis, FTA, and other risk prioritization tools can assist you and your organization in identifying and prioritizing risks. Reducing the likelihood of occurrence or the severity of the consequences of an unwanted risk (say, product failure) is a natural outcome of risk prioritization tools.

If it is not possible to reduce the occurrence or severity, then implementing controls is an option. Controls that either detect causes of unwanted events before the consequence occurs during product use, or that detect root causes of unwanted failures that the team can then avoid.

Controls may concentrate on management or decision-making processes. Improving the ability to detect design flaws or the accuracy of field failure rate prediction both improve the ability to make risk-appropriate decisions.

Diversification is another method for reducing or controlling risk. Thinking through the mix of products, technologies, markets, operations, and supply chains allows the team to limit the high-risk opportunities to a manageable or acceptable level.

Finally, unexpected events or high field failure rates will occur. Consider how you will detect the event's onset as well as how you will respond. It may be prudent to halt production and shipping when a single product failure has a significant impact (starting home on fire, for example). Make plans. Acting quickly and appropriately may reduce the risk of more failures/adverse consequences.

Transference

The goal of this strategy is to shift the burden of the risk consequence to another party. This may imply relinquishing some control, but if something goes wrong, your organization is not responsible.

If the product is associated with your organization, this approach may not work to protect your brand image. Even if the power supply vendor pays for all damages caused by failures in their unit, the customer only knows that your product failed and caused damage. Take this approach with caution.

Purchasing insurance is a traditional method of transferring risk to another organization. This may necessitate a careful examination of the risks and probabilities presented, but it is a viable option in some situations.

Contract terms with suppliers, vendors, contractors, and so on may provide a way to shift risk away from your organization. For example, if a power supply fails in an expensive server, resulting in revenue loss for a customer, you might request and receive a replacement power supply in most cases. Alternatively, you could require the power supply vendor to cover the cost of the entire server (which failed due to the power supply) as well as the customer's loss.

Risk Mitigation Strategies Synthesis

Avoid, accept, reduce/control, or transfer. You and your organization will have to deal with each risk you encounter. A little planning and effort open up more options than just a major product recall or bankruptcy filing.

Within your organization's risk management framework, you should be aware of the various strategies as well as understand the guidelines for their implementation.

Every day, engineers and managers across the organization make risk-related decisions. Providing a set of clear strategies as well as guidance allows the entire organization to appropriately mitigate risks daily.

Chapter 3

Risk Appetite Framework

For a firm to survive and expand into a financially viable operation, understanding the possible risks is vital.

A risk appetite framework is a management structure that helps firms identify their risks and how much they can absorb to meet their long and short-term objectives.

Learning about this method may help you build and apply it to your company endeavors. In this post, we define what risk and risk tolerance are, investigate the definition of RAF, evaluate who uses it, assess its essential components and study how to build one in five stages.

What is risk and risk tolerance in business? Risk is a specific impact or circumstance that may affect the good growth and development of a firm. Companies of all sizes have to cope with and handle specific risk issues at all phases of their life cycle.

The sort of hazards that a firm needs to handle typically depend on its sector. Danger tolerance is a statistic that evaluates how much risk a corporation can endure before they decide to interfere. Therefore, the lower a company's risk tolerance, the more likely they are to make safer selections. The greater their risk tolerance, the riskier their selections could be.

Here are some sorts of dangers that a firm might encounter:

Competitive risk
Most organizations have to fight the competitive risk, which characterizes a rival

firm acquiring the edge and making it tough for the business to fulfill its goals. For example, if two firms produce items of the same quality, the rival may be able to drive more track to their own company if they sell their products at a lesser price. A business should decide how many risks they are willing to take regarding their rivals since they make substantial modifications to acquire a competitive advantage.

Economic risk
This deals with the possible economic risk that might influence your firm. For example, factors in the economy can lead supplier costs to increase or your sales to decline. If there is any item that may generate a financial drop, it's likely an economic danger.

When dealing with this form of risk, a corporation may design measures to reduce any future losses and appraise how much financial risk they can take towards earning benefits.

Legal and compliance risk
Sometimes new rules and regulations might disrupt how a corporation runs. In turn, they may mistakenly even contravene these new rules or violate regulations because of an overlook of the modifications. This is a major concern for some firms that operate substantially within the limitations of their local and federal laws.

Therefore, they may construct an RAF to take those risks into mind so they can establish a threshold for what behaviors are allowed.

Reputation risk
A reputation or reputational risk indicates a loss in a company's reputation with customers and sometimes even its business partners. This form of risk might develop if the firm gets engaged in an occurrence or

practice that the general public or its target audience believes to be unfair, disrespectful, or dishonest. When a firm gets involved with this sort of danger, they may determine what habits or practices are no longer acceptable or they can decide what activities up to a certain extent they can absolve themselves of.

Security and fraud risk

This is a risk that is frequent within specific financial and information technology sectors and defines a company's susceptibility to possible security problems and fraudulent actions. A company that compiles databases of customer information has to be aware of the risk of hackers. This sort of problem may have a reduced risk tolerance to safeguard sensitive information.

What is a risk appetite framework?

A risk appetite framework describes the amount of risk a firm takes to accomplish its strategic goals and objectives. It's an inescapable component that certain choices and sectors are going to have inherent risks, but a corporation with appropriate tolerance may develop solutions to resolve those risks or work around them to attain their objectives.

The major objective of this framework is to assist enhance a company's risk awareness so it can identify and evaluate its risks properly. In turn, this empowers them to make more informed choices and develop a better and more active risk culture.

Ideally, a corporation should have a risk culture that balances risk awareness with risk-taking. Not enough risk can lead to the stagnation of innovation. Too much risk can cause a company to lose valuable resources or financial gains. Therefore, when creating a framework, a business must understand the nuances of its risks and use them to its advantage. For example, if a retailer has a competitor who offers the same product, then they can use the knowledge of that competitor's risk to be more innovative and create an item that might draw customers to their establishment.

Who uses a risk appetite framework?
Nearly every organization or institution, large or little, may adopt their interpretation of a risk appetite framework. This is because the essential objective of the structure stays the same, regardless of the risks or applied techniques being different.

For example, a bank could put in place particular risk management rules to regulate the impacts of security and fraud threats. They can accept these risks for a lengthy period or until the risk becomes too significant, at which point, the framework they have enables them to take more severe efforts to tackle the problem.

Here are just some of the entities that may employ risk appetite frameworks:

Corporations\sOrganizations
Academic institutions
Health and medical facilities
Banks
Legal firms
Retailers
Nonprofits and charities
Manufacturers

What does a risk appetite framework consist of?
Three basic components form a risk appetite framework, including:

Risk appetite statement
The risk appetite statement explains the relevant aspects surrounding the risks and delivers that information in a document. This statement serves as a management tool to guide leadership figures and employees on the amount of risk the company is

allowing itself to take on for the sake of pursuing critical objectives and goals.

As such, the statement helps the organization and staff members to make risk-informed decisions about the allocation of resources, potential impacts on other organizational departments, and management controls. The RAS serves to reduce any surprises or unforeseen losses since everyone is well-informed of the potential risks involved in their operations.

Risk capacity
In contrast to risk tolerance, risk capacity is a mandatory metric that describes two conditions. First, it describes how much risk a corporation has to take on to reach its goals. Second, It represents the highest amount of risk that the firm may accept before a breach of their existing finances and resources. This measurement generally refers to those inescapable and inherent business-related risks.

The rate of positive returns for the organization to reach its objectives considers numerous elements including resources required and key time frames to execute essential business tasks. You may then utilize your return rates to establish what the peak of your risk is. You define the objectives first before you can calculate the risk capacity necessary to achieve them.

Outline of roles

The overview highlights the staff personnel that are responsible for implementing and monitoring the risk appetite framework. Some firms employ hazard analysts, a risk manager, or a team of risk management professionals to undertake this responsibility. If these job roles do not exist within a company, then a leadership figure usually takes over the responsibility, like a security manager.

How to develop a risk appetite framework in 5 steps

Here are five steps to help you develop a comprehensive and useful risk appetite framework:

1. Define the company's strategic objectives and goals

The first step to do is to define what the targets are because there's a direct correlation between the company's goals and the RAF.

By emphasizing what the business hopes to achieve, you can better articulate how much risk the company is going to assume to reach those ambitions and bring them to fruition. A strategic plan provides a comprehensive detailing of the objectives and then further describes the individual benchmarks that are necessary to reach them successfully. When developing corporate objectives, aim to use the SMART approach, which communicates the following five concepts:

Exact: This explains the specific aim you intend to attain.
Measurable: This defines how you intend to measure your progress towards the objective.
Attainable: This defines how realistically you can reach the objective.
Relevant: This defines if the aim is valuable or relevant.
Timely: This defines when you intend to achieve the objective, like a deadline.

2. Create your risk appetite scale
After you have identified your company goals and objectives, the following step is to build a risk appetite scale. This tool helps you in particular the level of risk the company is going to assume to achieve the primary targets. Depending on the company, you may have to be cautious with your resources when working around one

type of risk, while you may have more freedom to be less conservative when managing another risk. The scaling approach enables you to assess how much risk tolerance you can accept for each danger.

Here is an instance of how you may identify your scale and then set your hazards under the proper section:

Risk seeking: Aggressive risk-taking is allowed.
Risk tolerant: Greater than normal risk-taking is tolerable.
Risk neutral: Risking taking is more balanced.
Moderately risk averse: Risk-taking should be more cautious.
Risk-averse: Assuming as little risk as possible is ideal.

3. Communicate with leadership and stakeholders

After the completion of the risk appetite scale, you must relay your information to the company leaders and stakeholders so you can get their input. Senior executives need to give their insight about their expectations and how much risk they believe the organization should take to reach the business goals.

As c-level team members, they have some ownership of how the company grows and runs. They can execute their responsibilities better and help the organization prosper when they offer their skills towards crucial business and risk management problems. You may further utilize their input to tweak the RAF as required.

4. Write your risk appetite statement

Writing a risk appetite statement is one of the most critical components of building a risk appetite framework because it describes the company's risk appetite succinctly and transparently to workers, leadership members, and stakeholders. This information helps anyone to make better educated and intelligent risk choices within the company's specified RAF. Therefore, when you create the RA statement, strive to utilize common and straightforward language that is easy to comprehend for everyone.

Refer to the language that the company has in their style manuals and documents to help you align your tone with the other enterprise materials.

5. Develop your tools for prioritization
Once everyone knows the RAF they can function within, and build the right tools that assist workers to prioritize their job as specified by the risk appetite. Support functions assist workers to bring key risk issues to the forefront and give them priority when required.

When staff has prioritization tools, they may make more educated daily choices that line with the company's risk appetite framework, such as understanding what investment decisions to make depending on where they lie on the risk appetite scale.

Chapter 4

Key Risk Indicator

Key Risk Indicators (KRIs) are key indicators of undesirable occurrences that might severely affect enterprises. They monitor changes in the degrees of risk exposure and contribute to the early warning indications that allow businesses to disclose hazards, avoid crises and manage them in time.

KRIs — separately or in combination with other risk environment-related data, such as loss occurrences, assessment findings, and problems — give important insights into the shortcomings within the risk and control environments.

They function as measurements of changes in an organization's risk profile, but given the evolving risk environment, merely defining them inside the corporate protocol may not be adequate.

Safeguarding a company against operational, reputational, and other risks needs frequent and regular evaluations of these KRIs. This assessment procedure also permits prompt notification of important hazards to the highest management.

All of this is feasible via an in-depth knowledge of risks which will allow accurate identification, construction of suitable risk indicators, and monitoring of performance regularly through the Key Performance Indicators (KPIs) while employing technology to support this process.

Characteristic Features of KRIs: KRIs are often quantifiable, i.e., they may be measured in terms of percentages, numbers, etc. They are predictable and are commonly utilized as early warning signals, while also monitoring patterns over some time. Since they give important insights regarding possible hazards that may affect corporate successes and objectives, KRIs are instructive and function as a catalyst for decision-making. Considering their significance, they must be built with care.

Designing Effective KRIs:\sDeveloping effective KRIs needs a deep knowledge of organizational goals and risk-related events that could impact the attainment of those objectives.

If the aim is to enhance profits by growing revenues and lowering expenses, a business may hone in on ways to accomplish this. But various possible dangers may arise which might damage any one or all of the tactics proposed. Mapping key risks to core strategic initiatives allows the management to identify the most critical metrics and monitor their performance. These measurements may assist supervise the execution of essential strategic goals and limit the likelihood of interruptions.

While most businesses monitor KRIs that have formed over time, they must be constantly reviewed for efficiency and continually monitored to indicate possible dangers. Over time, they must be reinforced with new KRIs to match the dynamic conditions as additional hazards develop and the earlier KRIs may be inadequate.

Having subject matter experts vet KRI designs will go a long way in keeping the business secure. They will be able to throw light on root cause events, stress spots, and intermediate events in their units or the processes they manage.

Their oversight may guarantee that critical risks are not neglected but are successfully disclosed at the correct moment, rather than after an undesirable occurrence has happened.

Effective KRIs are formed out of good quality data utilized to monitor a particular risk. The source of this data – internal or external to the company — must be checked and analyzed carefully.

This will go a long way in selecting the KRI to be applied. Sources like trade journals and talks with customers, staff, and members of the supply chain will give insights into the dangers they face that may be destructive to the business at an enterprise level.

Once the data is gathered, the methodologies utilized to measure and standardize KRIs must be consistent for the collated information to be robust and to make the decision process straightforward.

Relationship between KRIs and KPIs

One of the other most commonly used indicators in corporate governance is the KPIs or Key Performance Indicators. While the KRI is meant to warn of possible dangers, KPI assesses performance.

While many companies use them interchangeably, it is vital to differentiate between the two. KPIs are often meant to present a high-level picture of organizational performance. So although these indicators may not effectively give early warning signs of a rising problem, they are vital to examine trends and monitor performance. KRIs emphasize precisely the opposite.

KRIs can assist the management to comprehend developing risk exposures in many sections of the organization. At times, they represent critical ratios that the management may follow as indications of changing hazards, and prospective opportunities, which highlight the need for action. Others may be more complicated and incorporate the aggregate of numerous separate risk indicators into a multi-dimensional score concerning upcoming occurrences that may lead to new threats or opportunities.

For example, in the banking industry, a bank may construct a KPI that will contain statistics regarding defaulters. This KPI may identify an event that has already happened — a scenario where a customer failed on his payment to the bank as per his loan contract. However, building a KRI would be the more proactive technique to reveal loan repayment patterns before risk events occur.

To balance risks and opportunities effectively and to attain the greatest possible alignment of performance management and risk management, each KRI should be connected to a KPI. KPIs have traditionally played a vital role in performance management. And one of the most effective strategies to integrate performance and risk management is

Selecting KRIs, Setting Thresholds and Beyond2 To integrate risk factors into the company's performance management tool of choice. By integrating these, a company can measure and monitor performance and risk at the same time, as part of the same process.

Selecting KRIs, Setting Thresholds and Beyond2 Being proactive and pre-empting an undesirable circumstance from developing is generally achievable when the metrics to quantify the occurrence are well established. When picking KRIs, choose the ones that are quantifiable, meaningful, and predictive. Ensure that there are not too numerous, otherwise controlling them gets challenging. Select just those that give solid information. Once they are identified, firms should verify trigger levels and thresholds, set them based on their risk appetite and tolerance, or internal acceptability, and implement them after receiving an agreement from the Board of Directors.

Once the KRIs are in place, they must be monitored periodically — the frequency depends on what the KRI symbolizes. These should be reported to the highest management and escalation mechanisms must be devised and disclosed to workers managing these metrics.

Not all KRIs have the same degrees of escalation, therefore even if the organization escalates higher in a circumstance, it is vital to follow the hierarchy of reporting and not overload the management with too much information.

Challenges

While KRIs allow firms to resist risks and adversities, there are numerous factors behind why KRI monitoring also fails to produce economic benefits:

Difficulty in finding KRIs for all threats
Insufficient attention to the sources of the dangers
Failure to automate the collection of KRI values
Not using existing KPIs in conjunction with KRIs
Not associating actions with thresholds
But for each of these difficulties, there are corrective recommendations: businesses should start with the primary risks and then, extend.

They should assign KRIs for each reason. And as many KRIs as feasible should be automated to avoid them from growing stale. Existing KPIs should also be linked with the KRIs and both should be utilized to predict risks. Lastly, linking activities with thresholds goes a long way in synchronizing optimal thinking while creating thresholds.

Role of Technology in Effectively Measuring and Managing KRIs

Given the gains made by technology today, it is vital to harness it to look at multiple indicators in the context of the risk data being compiled for a company.

If the business is currently utilizing a risk management system, then it has its risk and control assessment data, and problem data, and can merge existing KRIs efficiently.

Technology allows the assessment of multiple risk categories, measurements, and even events. The system is not just for risks, it can also be used for asset classes, goals, controls, processes, business entities, etc. Once these are developed, one may construct thresholds (such as green, amber, and red) – which reflect increasing and lowering signs, both crucial and non-critical. Reporting and dashboards make it simple to detect crucial areas for analysis, thresholds – violated or otherwise.

Technology may be utilized to build a detailed tale when KRI levels climb. Automating KRIs to give them a longer life, monitoring corrective action when KRIs are escalated, track follow-ups – are some of the alternatives accessible when technology is harnessed.

Using technology also makes it simpler to explain to regulators the activities that are done, and the conditions that prompted them, as it provides an audit trail that discloses this information.

Risk management techniques may also be implemented for precise, quantifiable, relevant, and timely actions and responsibilities. Towards this end, it is vital to grasp KRI standards and measurement requirements. Furthermore, it is vital to discover the organization's analytics suppliers and the metrics consumers using different methods and resources.

One of the main advantages of employing technology to manage KRIs is that it does away with manual efforts, which can be time-consuming and burdensome. Technology allows human and automatic data collation techniques, allowing simple creation of thresholds, and records problems and actions for violations.

It gives a single interface to specify KRI, KPI, KCI (Key Control Indicators), and risk appetites. It is possible to monitor metrics for causes, repercussions, and hazards and they are readily available to workers researching these inside the company. It is also straightforward to tie KRIs, KPIs, and KCIs to anything in the organization's GRC collection of material.

To this end;
Designing and setting up KRIs is important to a successful ERM process. While the potential benefits of building a successful set of KRIs have been emphasized, it is equally vital to create the design components and procedures for their correct communication and flow within the realm of corporate governance.

KRIs in combination with the KPIs are believed to be efficient indicators of not only the possible dangers to a business but also how its divisions have been doing.

Though the difference is simply in perspective, an organization benefits far more when examining KPIs using risk lenses. It is believed that harnessing technology and leveraging it will only enhance organizations' risk management approach and complement existing risk identification methods to yield significant benefits.

Chapter 5

How to Manage Incentive

How do you do incentive management that motivates people to increase their job performance? When developing an incentive program, consider rewarded behaviors relevant to your workers as well as the company, and choose a period and pay kind that gets your people enthusiastic. If you don't, you might find yourself sponsoring a program that's ultimately a drain rather than a performance enhancer.

What is incentive management?
Incentive management is the process of delivering incentives like salary, additional time off, or a gift to workers who fulfill specified criteria or execute certain actions. A typical example of an incentive program is a system where a sales professional earns additional compensation for completing a

particular number of agreements in a quarter. Businesses develop incentive programs to promote and reinforce the behavior they seek from their staff.

But, incentive management isn't restricted to one-time cash incentives for sales personnel. Regardless of department, you may encourage incentives like an L&D incentive program with tuition reimbursement, awards for educational event attendance, or bonuses for strong scores on customer surveys.

Some business-wide examples include profit-sharing programs that contribute to the employee's retirement and performance recognition/reward programs that give recurring incentives.

Incentive management isn't restricted to one-time cash incentives for sales personnel.

Incentivize activities that fit with corporate and employee objectives
When you decide on behaviors to encourage in your incentive program, make sure they match up with your company's and your employees' objectives to guarantee they give high value and high impact.

Choose rewarded behaviors that complement your company goals
Define the outcomes you desire from your incentive program based on:

Corporate aims and values: Your incentive program's structure and recommended behaviors should correspond with company business objectives as well as company culture. Your program ought to speak to the principles you support in your day-to-day operations. For example, if your firm professes to support work/life balance, you don't want a program that rewards extra overtime.

Employee input: Employees typically offer recommendations for particular behaviors that may assist your team to attain broad-scope objectives, such as decreased rework for better job margin dollars. Since they work toward organizational goals every day, they could discover micro-trends that contribute to macro-trends.

Define goals that support staff growth
Now that you know the general objectives of your program, it's important to convert them into actionable actions for your staff. Effective incentive management goals inspire workers to accomplish their best by giving clear standards for them to fulfill that fit with your organization's present reality.

The SHRM official toolkit includes identifying quantifiable incentive behaviors, continuously assessing results, and altering your targeted behaviors as required to react to unanticipated events. You need metric-based benchmarks to establish whether your team members are attaining your program goals. But, you'll also want to keep an eye on those criteria and adjust them if they expand out of a fair scope for staff.

Set an incentive program scope that increases motivation
When you establish your incentive program's scope and participation, it'll become simpler to distribute your program resources and maintain them manageable for everyone involved, creating tough but attainable objectives for workers: the idea is to provide incentives that push people beyond their typical performance without making them seem out of reach.

Decide who will engage in your program and how
Some companies employ department-specific incentive schemes or systems that evaluate collective achievement above individual success. The ideal method

for your firm will rely on your team's OKRs and sources of incentive.

To evaluate whether you need a company-wide or group-specific program, review OKRs to search for organization-wide and department-wide trends. If you find people having problems meeting OKRs organization-wide, you may establish a company-wide program, and if you see an opportunity for growth in a single team or department, you can conduct the program on that level.

You should also evaluate whether you want to conduct a group incentive program across departments or groups inside a department, such as awarding sales teams for their collective quotas.

Some firms favor group reward schemes because they emphasize collaboration among team members over the competition. In addition, one research reveals that team-based incentives may boost performance by as much as 45% compared to individual programs' 27%.

Choose a short-term or long-term program
You'll also need to analyze whether your team requires a short-term campaign or an ongoing strategy to increase their performance under your incentive program.

According to a Namely research, the most typical periods for incentives are every year, every week, or on the spot. Psychology research says that more immediate incentives generate higher intrinsic motivation, so consider arranging your program to deliver a continual stream of prizes regardless of program duration.

Shorter award intervals may also help workers monitor their performance more regularly compared to yearly incentive periods.

Look at OKRs and KPI trends to evaluate whether performance requirements are current or continuing for program duration suggestions relevant to your staff.

A democratized needs analysis, which is where you engage team leaders about their team's performance requirements, may offer perspective to those figures.
Checking out OKRs can also disclose what intervals your staff uses to gauge their objectives so you can create timeframes that correspond.

Select a motivating and fair reward model
Incentive management compensation may go beyond financial awards. Whatever you pick, be sure to maintain your remuneration kind and structure reasonable and affordable for everyone.

Examples of incentive management compensation include:

Stocks\sPrizes
Flexible working possibilities
Redeemable points for time off or gifts
L&D opportunities
Office perks
Charitable gifts under the employee's name
According to an Incentive Research Foundation research, workers choose the time and experience-related benefits such as time off, flexible scheduling, and paid lunches/events.

They rated medals, free corporate items, and company-wide appreciation emails the lowest. Of course, every team has distinct values, so consider polling your staff to learn what they desire before you presume.

As you build your incentive plan, consider how much your remuneration will mean to various workers and add checks and balances to encourage fairness. Research demonstrates that the gender wage gap grows by 2% when incentives are incorporated. Considering that gender is only one inequity that leads to the wage gap, it's crucial to guarantee that workers of diverse demographics have appropriate incentives.

You may start creating equality in your incentive program by utilizing objective metrics and making sure that objectives are appropriate for everyone. For example, at some point companies eliminate wage bargaining for more fair pay—a concept you can apply to incentive management by concentrating on quantitative performance measurements.

You should keep individual skills and opportunities in mind as well, such as by assessing whether parents or persons with impairments might handle the scheduling commitment you ask for.

Incentive management is a collaborative effort

The most successful incentive programs are joint efforts involving leadership and staff. Take a communicative, bottom-up approach to incentive management where everyone is engaged in decision-making and offers frequent feedback on their experience. You could discover that dividing your incentive management power can increase your team's responsibility and dedication to their objectives

www.ingramcontent.com/pod-product-compliance
Lightning Source LLC
Chambersburg PA
CBHW061255140726
47998CB00006B/2224